MOTORING IN THE ISLE OF WIGHT.

Loading Motor Cars at Lymington.

The Transport of

MOTOR CARS BY RAILWAY

Services and Scales of Charges in 1914

*

Edited by

Peter R. Jenkins

Dragonwheel Books
1998

Printed and Published by Dragonwheel Books 1998
Sandcott Rectory Lane,
Pulborough,
West Sussex,
RH20 2AD

British Library C.I.P. Data:
A Catalogue Record is available from the British Library

ISBN   1 870177 37 1

TRANSPORT OF MOTOR CARS BY RAILWAY
Services and Scales of Charges, 1914

Motor cars for transport for Rail must be handed over to the Company uncharged with electricity, gas, oil, or other inflammable liquid or vapour (except as regards the small battery and coil usually fixed in petrol-propelled motor cars), and may be sent either by passenger or goods train services.

Cars must be handed over to the Company at the departure station, and taken over by the Consignors at the arrival station, unless a special arrangement as to collection or delivery is come to, for which, in every case, an extra charge varying with the circumstances would be made. The charge in London for such cartage is 10s. per ton with a minimum charge of 5s.

PASSENGER TRAIN SERVICES

The rate charged for motor cars by passenger train is 1s. 6d. per mile, calculated from station to station, the minimum charge being 7s. 6d., and the maximum weight per truck 50 cwt.

The Railway Companies accept no responsibility for cars sent at this rate. If it is desired to send cars at Company's risk, an extra charge of 25 per cent. is made; or insurance can be effected through the Railway Companies, at a premium of 1¼ per cent. of the actual value. Payment may be made either in advance or on delivery, but in the latter case the car will be deemed to have been carried at Owner's risk and uninsured, unless an understanding to the contrary was arrived at when arranging for the despatch of the car at the departure station. Motor cars sent at the above rates are carried on open trucks. If a covered truck is required, an extra charge of 5s. is made for distances up to 50 miles, 10s. for distances over 50 miles.

As a general rule, 24 hours' notice should be given when it is desired to send a motor car by passenger train, but in case of emergency this period can sometimes be reduced; for instance, notice might be given early in the morning for a car to be despatched by a train leaving on the evening of the same day.

There are no formalities in this connection beyond giving notice either verbally or in writing at the station from which the car is to be despatched.

Delivery can be had immediately the car is unloaded.

PRIVATE CARRIAGES, MOTOR CARS, ETC.,

CONDITIONS OF TRANSPORT BY PASSENGER TRAIN

(a) Private Carriages and Motor Cars sent on hire or for repairs, and Carriages and Motor Cars on loan sent to be used in place of other Carriages and Motor Cars under repairs.

(b) Private Carriages and Motor Cars sent on approval.

(c) Motor Chassis forwarded from Motor Works to Carriage Builders.

These are charged full rates on the outward journey, and if returned within three months, half-rates on the return journey at Owner's risk. Full rates at the Company's risk.

(d) Private Carriages, Motor Cars, and such Omnibuses as can be carried by Passenger Train, sent from one workshop to another (both workshops being the property of the same person or firm) are charged 25 per cent. less than the ordinary rates at Owner's risk. Full rates are charged at Company's risk.

(e) Old Private Carriages taken as part payment for, new Carriages are conveyed from the Owners to the Coachbuilders at half-rates at Owner's risk, provided they are both sent between the same points within three months. Minimum charge, 3s. 9d.

This reduction of 25 per cent. is not allowed in respect to carriages which are on the outward journey charged full rates, and half-rates on being returned within three months - see clauses (a), (b), and (c) above.

(f) Old Motor Cars exchanged for new Motor Cars carried from the Owners to the Makers, are charged half-rates at Owner's risk, provided they are both sent between the same points within three months, with a minimum charge of 3s. 9d.

(g) Private Carriages and Motor Cars sent from manufacturers to their Agents for sale are charge full rates.

A declaration stating that the vehicle is sent under the above-mentioned circumstances must be given by the sender in each case.

The minimum charges for vehicles sent under clauses (a), (b), and (c) above are 7s. 6d. for the outward journey, and 3s. 9d. for the return journey.

Motor Cars, minus the motor portion, are charged as Motor Cars.

Motor Tri-Cars, Mono-cars, or Duo-cars, are charged as Motor Cars.

Motor Car Bodies, without wheels, springs and motor portion, are charged as Carriages; not more than three being loaded on one truck.

When conveyed trucks are used for private carriages and Motor Cars conveyed under these arrangements, the full covered truck charge is made.

II. MOTOR BICYCLES AND TRICYCLES

Motor Cycles may be placed in the guards' van of a train by passengers when travelling, or consigned by the Railway Company for collection.

RATES FOR THE CARRIAGE OF

MOTOR BICYCLES

(by Passenger train)

Above:	And not exceeding:	Accompanied by Passenger Owner's risk.	Unaccompanied by Passenger Owner's risk	Company's risk
		s. d.	s. d.	s. d.
	12 miles	1 0	1 6	2 0
12 miles	25 miles	1 6	2 4	3 0
25 miles	50 miles	2 0	3 0	3 9
50 miles	75 miles	3 0	4 6	5 9
75 miles	100 miles	4 0	6 0	7 6
100 miles	150 miles	5 0	7 6	9 6
150 miles	200 miles	6 0	9 0	11 3
200 miles	250 miles	7 0	10 6	13 3
250 miles	300 miles	8 0	12 0	15 0
300 miles	350 miles	9 0	13 6	17 0
350 miles	400 miles	10 0	14 6	18 3
400 miles	450 miles	11 0	14 6	18 3
450 miles		12 0	14 6	18 3

RATES FOR THE CARRIAGE OF

MOTOR TRICYCLES

(By Passenger Train)

		Accompanied by Passenger Owner's risk.	Unaccompanied by Passenger Owner's risk	Company's risk
Above:	And not exceeding:	s. d.	s. d.	s. d.
	12 miles	2 0	3 0	3 9
12 miles	25 miles	3 0	3 9	5 6
25 miles	50 miles	4 0	5 0	7 0
50 miles	75 miles	6 0	7 6	10 0
75 miles	100 miles	8 0	10 0	13 6
100 miles	150 miles	10 0	12 6	16 6
150 miles	200 miles	12 0	15 0	19 6
200 miles	250 miles	14 0	17 6	23 0
250 miles	300 miles	16 0	20 0	26 0
300 miles	350 miles	18 0	22 0	29 0
350 miles	400 miles	20 0	24 0	32 0
400 miles	450 miles	22 0	26 0	35 0
450 miles		24 0	28 0	38 0

Motor Cycles must be uncharged with electricity, gas, oil, or other inflammable liquid or vapour (except as regards the small electric battery and coil usually fixed to petrol-propelled Motor Cycles), when conveyed in the guard's van of passenger trains.

A passenger may take no more than two Motor Bicycles or Motor Tricycles at the Accompanied rate when travelling. They are not accepted at Company's risk.

The rates for Unaccompanied Motor Bicycles or Motor Tricycles do not include charges for collection and delivery.

A Motor Bicycle minus the engine and tank is charged at the full rate for the class of machine.

UNACCOMPANIED LUGGAGE BY RAILWAY

Motorists desiring to send ordinary luggage, such as trunks, boxes, etc., by Rail, unaccompanied, may do so (Channel Islands excepted) at the usual parcel rates, which in England, vary from:

4d. per 1lb., up to 30 miles, to 6s. 6d. per 100lbs. per 100 miles.

The intermediate and Irish rates can be obtained from the respective Railway Companies.

GOODS TRAIN SERVICES

The rates for conveyance of motor cars by goods train are given in the table below. This list is subject to alteration by the Railway Companies without notice at any time.

Cars sent at these rates are conveyed at the Railway Company's risk.

Motor cars are accepted for conveyance by goods train without previous notice, but it is preferable to give notice to enable a suitable truck to be provided.

The rates are for transport of a single motor car on an open carriage truck. For the use of a covered truck, of passenger or goods construction, for the conveyance of any vehicle, an additional charge of 10s. will be made.

The time in transit of course varies according to the distance covered; but it may be taken as a general rule that except for very long distances, motor cars will arrive at destination on the day after their despatch.

Motor cars for conveyance by goods train are accepted at all goods stations, where facilities are provided for their loading. They are not accepted at purely passenger stations for conveyance at goods rates.

Carriage charges can be may payable by either the consignor or the consignee. In the first instance, the charges should be paid when the traffic is tendered; in the latter, when delivered.

In the case of traffic to London, the mileage rates listed in the table are applicable only to the stations of the Railway Company carrying the traffic into London, and not beyond to any other London station.

RATES FOR CARRYING AUTOMOBILES
(unpacked)
BY GOODS TRAIN
(Station to Station)

For any distance not over	Rate per ton Minimum 1 ton		For any distance not over	Rate per ton Minimum 1 ton		For any distance not over	Rate per ton Minimum 1 ton	
Miles	s.	d.	Miles	s.	d.	Miles	s.	d.
10	7	7	230	76	2	450	134	10
20	12	7	240	78	10	460	137	6
30	17	7	250	81	6	470	140	2
40	22	7	260	84	2	480	142	10
50	27	7	270	86	0	490	145	6
60	30	6	280	89	6	500	148	2
70	33	3	290	92	2	510	150	10
80	36	0	300	94	10	520	153	6
90	38	0	310	97	6	530	156	2
100	41	6	320	100	2	540	158	10
110	44	2	330	102	10	550	161	6
120	46	10	340	105	6	560	164	2
130	49	6	350	108	2	570	166	10
140	52	2	360	110	10	580	169	6
150	54	10	370	113	6	590	172	2
160	57	6	380	116	2	600	174	10
170	60	2	390	118	10	510	177	6
180	62	10	400	121	6	620	180	2
190	65	6	410	124	2	630	182	10
200	68	2	420	126	10	640	185	6
210	70	10	430	129	6	650	188	2
220	73	6	440	132	2			

For use of a Covered Truck, Passenger or Goods, for the conveyance of any vehicle, an additional charge of 10s. is made.

RAILWAY FERRY, Etc., SERVICES

Greenock - Helensburgh (North British Railway Co, ferry service)
No Sunday service. Cars cannot be shipped at low tide.
Fares.
Passengers: Cabin, single, 6d.; return, 1s. Steerage, single, 6d.; return, 10d.
Cars: up to 15 cwt., 1s. per cwt.; 15 - 30 cwt., £1; 6d. per cwt. over 30 cwt.
Motor Cycles: 6d.

Greenock - Kilmum (G.& S.W.R. ferry service)
No Sunday service. Fares as above.

Hull - New Holland (G.C.R. ferry service)
Week-day service connecting with trains to and from New Holland (weather permitting). First boat leaves Hull at 5.40a.m., last boat leaves New Holland at 10.20p.m. On Saturdays a late boat leaves Hull at 11.05p.m. and New Holland at 11.30p.m. Large cars can only be taken at High Tide, and notice should be given if possible. Petrol tanks must be emptied.
Fares.
Passengers: Deck, single, 4d.; return, 8d. Saloon, single, 6d., return, 11d.
Ordinary Cars: Owner's risk, 5s.; Company's risk, 10s.
Cars less than 10 feet long and under 11 cwt.: O.R., 3s. 6d.; C.R., 7s.
Motor Cycles: Owners's risk, 6d., Company's risk, 7½d.

Portsmouth - Ryde (L.& S.W. and L.B.& S.C. Joint ferry service.)
By steam packet tow boats, from Portsmouth (Broad St. slipway) at 8.45a.m. and 1p.m., and from Ryde (George St. slipway) at 10a.m. and 3p.m., tide and weather permitting. No service on Sundays and public holidays. Vehicles are only accepted at Owner's risk.
Fares.
Passengers (only taken in tow boats in fine weather, and recorded as 'persons in charge'): 6d. each.
Cars and Cycle-cars: Up to 10 cwt., 9s.; over 10cwt., 14s.
Motor Cycles: 1s.6d.
Motor Tricars: 5s.
Motor Cycle with Side-car or Motor Tricycle: 3s.

Lymington Town Station Wharf - Yarmouth (L.& S.W.R. ferry service.)
By tow boats on week days and Bank Holidays, except Christmas Day and Good Friday. Cars should be upon the wharf half an hour before sailing times. A few hours' notice should be given to the station master at Yarmouth. Motor cycles can be conveyed by passenger boat if their petrol tanks are emptied. This is not necessary for the motor car service.
Fares. (A Sunday sailing can be arranged at an extra charge of £1.)
Passengers: Third class single, 1s. 6d.
Cars: up to 10cwt., single, 9s. return, 15s.; over 10cwt., 14s. and 25s.
Motor Cycles: 1s. 6d.

River Severn (G.W.R. train service by Severn Tunnel.)
Pilning station and Patchway station to Severn Tunnel Junction. Daily service. Petrol tanks must be emptied, but an equivalent amount is given at the other end on presentation of a voucher from the forwarding station. Cars must be at the station half-an-hour before the train is due to start, and 24 hours notice must be given if a covered truck is required.
Fares from Pilning.
Passengers: First class 2s. 4d.; Third class 1s. 2d.
Cars or Cycle-cars on Open Trucks at Owner's risk: 7s. 6d.
- in Covered Carriage Trucks at Owner's risk: 12s. 6d.
- in Covered Carriage Trucks at Company's risk: 14s. 5d.
Fares from Patchway.
Passengers: First class 3s. 0d.; Third class 2s. 4d.
Cars or Cycle-cars on Open Trucks at Owner's risk: 9s. 0d.
- in Covered Carriage Trucks at Owner's risk: 14s. 0d.
- in Covered Carriage Trucks at Company's risk: 16s. 3d.

River Severn (G.W. & Midland Joint Railway train service by Severn Bridge.)
Sharpness station to Lydney Town station. No trains on Sundays, Christmas Day, and Good Friday. Petrol tanks must be emptied.
Fares.
Passengers: First class 1s. 3d.; Third class 7½d.
Cars: 7s. 6d. at Owner's risk.
Motor Cycles, accompanied by passenger: 1s. at Owner's risk.
Motor Tricycles, accompanied by passenger: 2s. at Owner's risk.

RAILWAY COMPANY STEAMSHIP SERVICES

Motor Cars, Motor Bicycles, etc., are accepted for transport by several routes.

GREAT CENTRAL RAILWAY

Grimsby - Antwerp, Hamburg, and Rotterdam

Cars should be at the Royal Hotel Garage, Grimsby Docks, not later than noon on the day of sailing. Boats leave Grimsby soon after the arrival of the boat train at 6.45p.m. On Sundays, cars cannot be landed in Hamburg; cars may be landed at Antwerp, Rotterdam and Grimsby on Sundays at no extra charge if notice is given by noon on Saturday.

GREAT EASTERN RAILWAY

Harwich - Antwerp and Hook of Holland

Garaging is provided at Parkeston Quay for a charge of 2s. per night. The G.E.R. reserves the right to alter rates and charges without giving notice, except as provided by the Railway and Canal Traffic Act, 1888.

GREAT WESTERN RAILWAY

Fishguard - Wexford, Waterford and Cork

Weymouth - Channel Islands

Holders of return tickets to Jersey may break their journey at Guernsey both ways without extra charge.

LANCASHIRE & YORKSHIRE RAILWAY

Goole - Antwerp and Hamburg

Liverpool - Drogheda

Fleetwood - Belfast (L.& Y. and L.& N.W. Joint Railway Co.)

Hull - Zeebrugge (L.& Y. and N.E. Joint Railway Co.)

LONDON & NORTH WESTERN RAILWAY

Holyhead - Dublin, North Wall

Holyhead - Greenore

Cars should be at Holyhead at least 2½ hours before the time of sailing. On the Dublin route motor cars are conveyed by cargo boat on which there is no First class saloon accommodation. No Sunday sailngs to Greenore.

LONDON, BRIGHTON & SOUTH COAST RAILWAY
Newhaven - Dieppe

Cars shipped by cargo boats cannot be cleared by Customs on Sundays. Insurance at Lloyds at the rate of 2s. 5d. per £100 value may be obtained. Motor Cycles may be sent at from any station on the L.B.& S.C.R. which accepts baggage for Dieppe.

LONDON & SOUTH WESTERN RAILWAY
Southampton - Cherbourg

Southampton - Havre

Southampton - St. Malo

Southampton - Channel Islands

At least 12 hours notice of shipment is required, with full particulars of the car and the expected time of its arrival on the quay. Petrol tanks will be emptied at Southampton by the Company's Motor Attendant. An extra charge of 5s. is made for cars landing at Southampton on Sunday, and at Cherbourg a charge of 12frs. 10c. is made for unloading at low tide, when a steam-crane is necessary. Shippers may insure cars at the rate of 5s. per £100 value upon giving 12 hours notice.

MIDLAND RAILWAY
Heysham - Belfast

Heysham - Dublin

Heysham - Douglas

SOUTH EASTERN & CHATHAM RAILWAY
Dover - Calais

Transport by night cargo boat only. Special through rates apply between Victoria and Calais, for cars on their own wheels or packed in crates. Unpacked cars should be handed in at Victoria station. Twenty-four hours should be given of embarkation at Dover or Calais. Cars awaiting embarkation at Calais should be placed in the charge of the S.E.& C.R. Company's Agent. Motors must not be charged with electricity, oil, or fuel.

Folkestone - Boulogne

Cars may be shipped by passenger boat on this route.

Queenborough and Folkestone - Flushing